Surviving
a Tornado

by Heather Adamson

amicus readers

2

amicus readers

Say hello to amicus readers.

You'll find our helpful dog, Amicus, chasing a ball—to let you know the reading level of a book.

A

Learn to Read

Frequent repetition of sentence structures, high frequency words, and familiar topics provide ample support for brand new readers. Approximately 100 words.

1

Read Independently

Repetition is mixed with varied sentence structures and 6 to 8 content words per book are introduced with photo label and picture glossary supports. Approximately 150 words.

2

Read to Know More

These books feature a higher text load with additional nonfiction features such as more photos, time lines, and text divided into sections. Approximately 250 words.

Amicus Readers are published by Amicus
P.O. Box 1329, Mankato, Minnesota 56002
www.amicuspublishing.us

Printed in the United States of America at at Corporate
Graphics, in North Mankato, Minnesota.

Series Editor   Rebecca Glaser
Series Designer   Bobbi J. Wyss
Photo Researcher   Heather Dreisbach

Library of Congress Cataloging-in-Publication Data
Adamson, Heather, 1974-
  Surviving a tornado / by Heather Adamson.
    p. cm. – (Amicus Readers. Be prepared)
  Includes index.
  Summary: "Discusses the dangers of tornados, how
to prepare for them, and how to stay safe during and
after a tornado"–Provided by publisher.
  ISBN 978-1-60753-152-4 (library binding)
  1. Tornadoes–Juvenile literature. 2. Tornadoes–Safety
measures–Juvenile literature. I. Title.
  QC955.2.A33 2012
  613.6'9–dc22
                                        2010042153

Photo Credits
GENE RHODEN/Photolibrary, cover; Getty Images, 1; A. T. Willett/Alamy, 5, 20m; Mike Hollingshead/Getty Images, 6; AFP/Getty Images, 7, 20t; Tammy Bryngelson/iStockphoto, 9; Heather King, Virginia Department of Emergency Management, 10, 21t; Peng Zhangqing/XinHua/Xinhua Press/Corbis, 11; David R. Frazier Photolibrary, Inc./Alamy, 13, 20b; FEMA/Leif Skoogfors, 14, 21bm; FEMA/Charles S. Powell, 15, 21t; Jim West/Alamy, 17; Ron Buskirk/Alamy, 19; NOAA/NWS, 21b; RonTech2000/iStockphoto, 22a; proxyminder/iStockphoto, 22b; Chris Bence/iStockphoto, 22c

1035   3-2011
10 9 8 7 6 5 4 3 2 1

Table of Contents

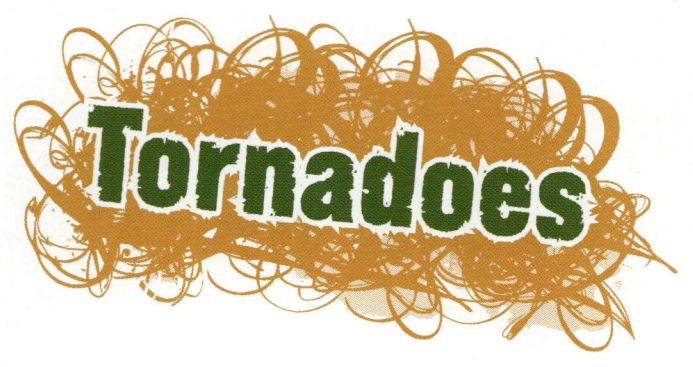

Tornadoes

Storm clouds twist when warm air and cold air meet. They form into dangerous tornadoes that look like giant funnels. Wild **funnel clouds** throw things in the air.

funnel cloud

Tornadoes knock down houses and trees. People can get hurt from this flying **debris**. You can stay safe if you are prepared.

debris

Be Prepared

You can plan how to survive a storm. Find a safe place in your home. Go to the lowest part of the building.

Stairwells, closets, and bathrooms can be safe places. They are sturdy to block debris. They have few windows.

Practice getting to your safe place with a **tornado drill**. Go to the safe area and get down low. Cover your head with your hands or something hard.

At school, follow your teacher's directions to get to a safe place.

tornado drill

10

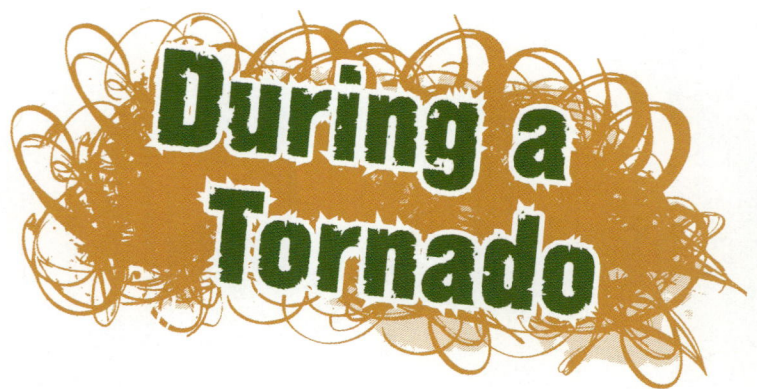

During a Tornado

When the weather might get stormy, **meteorologists** announce tornado watches.

A **tornado watch** means the weather could change into a bad storm.

A **tornado warning** sounds when a tornado is near.

meteorologist

Loud sirens let people know a tornado has been spotted.

If you hear a storm siren, go to a safe place. Big buildings may have **shelters** built in. Most gyms and mobile homes are not safe. The roofs blow off and the walls fall in. If you can't find a safe place, lay down outside.

shelter

After a Tornado

When the storm has
stopped, come out carefully.
Tornadoes whip debris,
but they also tip and shake
buildings. There can be
cracks or problems you
don't see right away. Let
someone check to be sure
the building is still safe.

Tornadoes can make a big mess. It may take a while to clean up and rebuild what tornadoes wreck. You cannot stop a tornado, but you can stay safe.

Photo Glossary

debris
pieces of broken things that blow around during a tornado

funnel cloud
a cone-shaped cloud that is wide at the top

meteorologist
someone who studies the earth's climate and weather

shelters
special buildings or parts of buildings that have been built strong enough to take storms

tornado drill
practicing what to do if there is a tornado

tornado warning
when a tornado is spotted near your area; storm sirens sound in a warning.

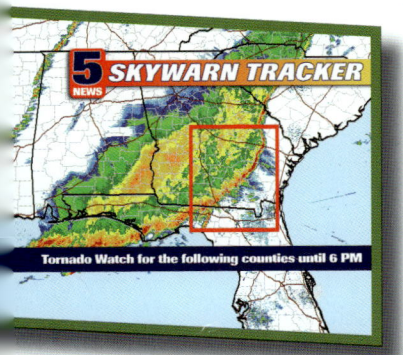

tornado watch
when the weather conditions might create severe storms or tornadoes

Activity: Safe Places in a Tornado

Where is a safe place to go in a tornado?

1 and 3 are safe places. #1 is away from windows. #3 is the lowest level of a house. #2 is not a safe place to be in a tornado. Gym roofs usually blow off in a tornado.

Ideas for Parents and Teachers

Be Prepared, an Amicus Readers Level 2 series, provides simple explanations of what storms are and offers reassuring steps that kids and families can take to be prepared for disasters. As you read this book with your children or students, use the ideas below to help them get even more out of their reading experience.

Before Reading

* Read the title and ask the students if they've ever experienced a tornado or know someone who has.

* Ask the students if they know what to do during a tornado.

* Use the photo glossary words to help them predict what they will learn from the book.

Read the Book

* Ask the students to read the book independently.

* Provide support where necessary. Show students how to use the photo glossary if they need help with words.

After Reading

* Ask the students to retell what they learned about preparing and staying safe during tornadoes. Compare their answers to what they said before reading the book.

* Have students do the activity on page 22 and talk about how they would prepare for a storm. Hold a tornado drill in your home or school.

Index

Web Sites

FEMA for Kids—Disaster Connection
http://www.fema.gov/kids/tornado.htm

Ready Kids—Be Prepared in Every Situation
http://www.ready.gov/kids/home.html

Red Cross of Central Illinois—Tornado Safety Video
https://www.redcrossillinois.org/tornado-safety-tips

Weather Wiz Kids—Tornado Information
http://www.weatherwizkids.com/weather-tornado.htm